1 MONTH OF FREE READING

at

www.ForgottenBooks.com

By purchasing this book you are eligible for one month membership to ForgottenBooks.com, giving you unlimited access to our entire collection of over 1,000,000 titles via our web site and mobile apps.

To claim your free month visit: www.forgottenbooks.com/free816079

* Offer is valid for 45 days from date of purchase. Terms and conditions apply.

ISBN 978-0-365-20443-5
PIBN 10816079

This book is a reproduction of an important historical work. Forgotten Books uses state-of-the-art technology to digitally reconstruct the work, preserving the original format whilst repairing imperfections present in the aged copy. In rare cases, an imperfection in the original, such as a blemish or missing page, may be replicated in our edition. We do, however, repair the vast majority of imperfections successfully; any imperfections that remain are intentionally left to preserve the state of such historical works.

Forgotten Books is a registered trademark of FB &c Ltd.
Copyright © 2018 FB &c Ltd.
FB &c Ltd, Dalton House, 60 Windsor Avenue, London, SW19 2RR.
Company number 08720141. Registered in England and Wales.

For support please visit www.forgottenbooks.com

AMERICAN HISTORICAL ASSOCIATION.

THE TEACHING OF HISTORY.

BY

HERBERT B. ADAMS, Ph. D., LL. D.,
OF JOHNS HOPKINS UNIVERSITY.

(From the Annual Report of the American Historical Association for 1896
Vol. I, pages 243-263.)

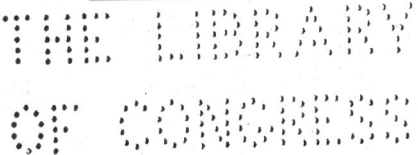

WASHINGTON:
GOVERNMENT PRINTING OFFICE.
1897.

FEB 3 1903
D. of D.

XII.—THE TEACHING OF HISTORY.

By HERBERT B. ADAMS, Ph. D., LL. D.,
OF JOHNS HOPKINS UNIVERSITY

THE TEACHING OF HISTORY.

By HERBERT B. ADAMS.

In 1896 I spent my entire summer vacation in Great Britain, Ireland, and Scotland visiting university towns and attending so-called "Summer meetings," or summer schools, of which I have been making a study for the United States Bureau of Education. At Old Chester there was a meeting of the National Home Reading Union, corresponding to the American "Chautauqua." This union now embraces thousands of readers and is under the practical guidance of some of the best university men in England. Dr. Mandel Creighton, the newly appointed Bishop of London, gave the opening address on "The moral aspect of history." Other historical lectures were given by Cambridge men and Girton women; also talks on English architecture by eminent specialists, with Chester Cathedral and the Cistercian Abbey of Valle Crucis for class rooms and object lessons. Excursions were made to ancient castles and places of historical interest near Chester. The town itself with its ancient walls, quaint architecture, and Roman survivals, Hawarden and Conway Castles, Offa's Dike, and the whole country round were open books for the teaching of history.

The same was true of Old Cambridge, where University Extension students and teachers assembled from all parts of England, with guests from Belgium, Germany, Austria, Denmark, and Scandinavia. History was taught not only in class rooms, but by the associations and architecture of the place. One of the most interesting courses of historical lectures delivered at the Cambridge Summer Meeting was upon the subject of the Dissolution of the Monasteries. What a striking object lesson of monastic spoliation and transformation was afforded by those Cambridge colleges. For example: (1) Trinity, the noblest college of them all, founded upon nine earlier religious establishments; (2) Jesus College, whose very buildings once belonged to a Benedictine nunnery; (3) Sidney-Sussex (the college of Cromwell), built on the site of a Franciscan monastery, the Grey Friars; (4) Emmanuel (the alma mater of John Harvard, the first university extensioner in the New World), erected on the very spot where the Dominicans or Black Friars lived and preached until dispossessed by that arch spoilsman, Henry VIII; (5) St. Mary Magdalene College, on ground once occupied by the Monks' Hostel of the Benedictine students from Croyland Abbey; (6) Peterhouse, the oldest college in Cambridge and an institutional offshoot of the bishopric of Ely. Think of an historical excursion to that old cathedral town, with lectures and peripatetic talks by the dean and his canons on the very premises of the Benedictines! That was a kind of history teaching which I had never before enjoyed, and I gladly recommend it to American students and instructors who would like to vary their pedagogical experience.

In alternate years the Summer Meeting is held at Oxford, which is perhaps even richer than Cambridge in historic associations. At these summer gatherings Americans hear and meet some of the best historical teachers and lecturers in England and come home, as I did, with enlarged views of public educational duty and of modern university opportunities. It is not enough to teach history to college boys and girls. It must be taught to school teachers and to the American people. The campaign before this American democracy is educational, moral, and religious. History, politics, and economics, with religion, ethics, music, art, good literature, good newspapers, good public speaking, and good, popular lecturing will be among the winning forces. Churches, libraries, school boards, colleges, and universities must all enter the open field of missionary labor for the public good, the salus publica.

At the Edinburgh Summer Meeting I was most interested, pedagogically, in the remarkable attempt to combine political and natural science, sociology and biology, history and geography, zoology and botany. Prof. Patrick Geddes and his colleagues are actually succeeding in this combination. Dr. Wenley, a professor of philosophy lately called from Glasgow to the University of Michigan, lectured on the relation between science and philosophy. Mr. Branford discussed the "Comparative Economics of Europe from the standpoint of natural history."

Some years ago I called attention to the original association of civil history with natural history in the ancient curriculum of Harvard College. That idea, which I once thought absurd, has been actually realized every summer at Edinburgh during the past ten years by Professor Geddes, whose lectures on "Contemporary Social Evolution" combined biology and history. His course on "Scotland, historic and actual," was another study in social evolution, combining in a most interesting and suggestive way physical geography and ethnography with historical sociology. Professor Geddes laid great stress in his familiar teaching upon historic survivals and their interpretation—upon the survey of regional environments like that of the historic city of Edinburgh and the neighboring kingdom of Fife. He was fond of taking his classes to the Outlook Tower on Castle Hill at Edinburgh and there pointing out object lessons in the physical and political history of Scotland. He led a series of excursions to places combining biological and social interest. Often would he replace the formal lecture of the class room by demonstration from actual and visible objects. For him the old town of Edinburgh, King Arthur's country, Melrose and Dryburgh abbeys, Roman walls, Stirling Castle, the fiords, lakes, islands, hills of Scotland, and even the Caledonian Canal were not only picturesque phenomena, but good illustrations of history, politics, economics, and sociology. Professor Geddes believes that "knowledge must always grow from the things and facts familiar and at hand to those far off and recondite." He does not believe in "proceeding from a past which the pupil has no means of realizing toward a present which he never reaches at all." He says: "It is through the vivid endeavor to comprehend the present that we are impelled toward the reconstruction and interpretation of the past."

In this connection as a teacher of history I should like to explain that I have never taught that all history is past politics and that all politics are present history, but only that some history and some politics are thus defined. It must be fully recognized that history is past religion, past philosophy, past civilization, past sociology, and includes all man's recorded action and experience in organized society; but for practical and working purposes we may adopt any historical motto that we like. There is a sense in which the dictum of the late Professor Freeman is true, and it is recognized by some of the best scholars in England and Germany. Lord Acton, the successor of Prof. J. R. Seeley at Cambridge, said in a public lecture that a student of history "is the politician with his face turned backward." He quotes with manifest approval a German saying: "Die Geschichte ist derselbe Janus mit dem Doppelgesicht, das in der Geschichte, in die Vergangenheit, in der Politik in die Zukunft hinschaut." Droysen used to say: "What is politics to-day becomes history to-morrow." Professor Maurenbrecher, at Leipzig, in his inaugural address, while recognizing that there are other fields of historical interest and inquiry beside the State—for example, the church, religion, art, and science—maintains that history proper is political history, for without law and government there can be no culture or civilization. History reaches its goal in politics and politics are always the resultant of history. The two subjects are related like past and present.[1] The subject of historic evolution would have no vital interest unless the past was in some way related to the present. "History made and history making," says Lord Acton, "are scientifically inseparable and separately unmeaning."

Twenty years ago I was an advocate of local history. I then believed in an American approaching the great field of the world's historic life from the vantage ground of local interest. I taught my students to some extent the local history of New England, e. g., of Plymouth Plantations, of Salem and the Massachusetts Bay towns as typical of the English mode of settlement and as illustrative of the continuity of Germanic common land tenure and village institutions in the New World. The idea proved stimulating to similar studies in various parts of the country, North and South; but I early discovered that there was not sufficient historic training and positive knowledge on the part of the average college or university student to justify the devotion of very much time to local studies on the part of either teacher or pupil.

While I am still an advocate, for patriotic and other reasons, of American graduate students in their own country choosing for the most part American subjects for historical research, I believe that an American teacher of history should not lead his class prematurely, by lectures or seminary exercises, into

---

[1] For a fuller discussion of "History and Politics," see Proceedings of the Sixth Annual Meeting of the Association of Colleges and Preparatory Schools in the Middle States and Maryland, 1894: "Is History Past Politics?" By H. B. Adams.

local, State, or even national byways of specialized historical inquiry. In short, my present conviction is that a long period of college and university study, say, four or five years, in general history, should precede specialization in local history or American history. I have been acting upon this conviction in department work at the Johns Hopkins University, where for a long time fully two-thirds of both collegiate and graduate work in history has been upon Old World ground rather than upon New World territory. The college or university teacher, it seems to me, should seek to give his pupils a proper background of English, European, classical, and Oriental history before allowing them to specialize in the history of their country.

Of course this preliminary training can not usually be given by one teacher. The work properly involves a division of labor and an organized department. But sometimes it is necessary, for financial and other reasons, for one college professor or teacher of history to represent the whole subject of human history. Under such circumstances I think he would better represent it by giving preliminary courses in general history, or the history of civilization, than he would by confining the attention of his class to the narrower fields of French, German, English, or American history, whether local or national.

Many of us remember the old-time limitations of college work in history, and think with gratitude of those broad and comprehensive courses of instruction that were given by individual teachers like Professors Diman, Stillé, White, Torrey, and Allen. About all the history that students learned in those days was through the medium of general lecture courses or Guizot's History of Civilization. It is a gratifying evidence of the permanent value of such methods of general instruction that excellent text-books on European history and civilization have been written by well-known members of this Association. A recent American work of this kind is Prof. G. P. Fisher's History of the Nations and of their Progress in Civilization.

I have found that one of the best ways of teaching collegiate students general history is by the well-worn and ancient paths of Jewish and church history. Starting with Chaldæan and old Babylonian civilization, one can show the kinship of Hebrew and Semitic ideas and institutions. Phœnician and Egyptian civilizations may be reviewed and the points of contact with Israel clearly noted. The contributions of Israel's neighbors to Jewish civilization and to world history should be tabulated in thesis form by members of the class and fortified by citations from private reading.

This method of undergraduate training in the historical sociology of the Hebrews involves to a certain extent the actual use of original sources of Hebrew literature, and at the same time an acquaintance with matters of general human interest about which American college graduates know far too little. A mayor of Baltimore was once called upon to give an address on the rededication of a Methodist Episcopal Church (colored) called "The Ebenezer Church." The pious mayor, wishing to testify to his familiarity with the Old Testament as well as his general sympathy with the colored voters, said: "Men and brethren: I have always had the greatest respect for that old Hebrew patriarch Ebenezer." The best of this joke is that it is obscure (I Sam. vii, 12) and needs a concordance or a commentary. I have told the story to many college students and some professors, and am always gratified if anybody sees the point.

Some persons may object to this Baltimore story about Ebenezer as local history, but surely it is worth while to teach a class of boys that "Ebenezer" was a rude stone altar erected to the Lord on a battlefield where the Philistines were driven backward. It illustrates the historic origin of many a sacred *menhir* or monumental column from ancient Palestine to the Pillars of Hercules. It is worth while for liberally educated college students to learn something of the fundamental institutions of the Shemites, as taught by such men as Robertson Smith and George Adam Smith, "the two Smiths" who have so enlightened modern Scotland that trials for heresy are no longer possible there, as they still are in our own country. Last summer when I was in Scotland, a theological professor was retired from office by the constituted authorities because he knew nothing of the higher criticism and the students would no longer listen to him.

There is a perfectly safe way of illuminating the modern student's mind without destroying his religious faith. That way lies through Hebrew literature, social and institutional history. The higher critics have about accomplished their work. Joseph Jacobs, in his "Studies in Biblical Archæology" (XII), says: "Literary criticism seems now to have come to an end of its tether with regard to the 'slicing' of the Hexateuch;

the reconstructions of Genesis by Fripp and Bacon, and of the whole Hexateuch by Addis, and the exhaustive work of Holzinger, all serve to show this. They all confirm my contention that on this line of research we can not further go. Literary search per se can not solve the problem of the Hexateuch, so far as that problem is concerned with the development of institutions of the ancient Hebrews."

Recently I have endeavored to so broaden and deepen my course in Hebrew history that it might gradually become a means of reviewing various Oriental religions. This year I began with Confucianism and Shintooism in China and Japan and continued with Brahminism and Buddhism in India. From this Asiatic background my class approached Judaism and Christianity.

Church history is a general course of liberalizing and illuminating college study, and one of the best introductions to the history of mediæval and modern Europe. The subject is usually monopolized by theological seminaries, where it is sometimes taught in a very narrow way. It ought to be taught not as the history of councils, creeds, and heresies, but as the institutional exponent of Christian civilization, in which the mediæval and modern world live and move and have their being. Lord Acton agrees with Bishop Stubbs in the view that "Modern history, including mediæval history in the term, is coextensive in its field of view, in its habits of criticism, in the person of its most famous students, with ecclesiastical history." With this great subject naturally belong the history of art and education and the historic relations between civil and ecclesiastical society, which find their best and highest expression in America, where a free church in a free State has become an institutional reality. This is, perhaps, America's greatest and most original contribution to history and political science.

The beginning and the end of historical evolution are the most interesting things to study and teach. A former president of this Association, Henry Adams, once said: "There is no history left for Americans to write except that of the North American Indians and the twentieth century." Although somewhat satirical, this remark implies a certain truth. All history begins with savagery and ends, like the story of the Jews and of the Christian Church, in prophetic ideals—in visions of things to come.

American teachers of history have a singular advantage of being able, within the limits of their own country, to illustrate the beginning and the end of historic evolution. The ethnological researches of Major Powell and his associates have taught us that the rudimentary forms of religion and government may be studied in the folklore and tribal customs of the North American Indians. Last summer, at the University of Edinburgh, I met M. Reclus, an eminent authority in the field of comparative religion, and he assured me that the historical world owes a great debt to Major Powell and the United States Government for encouraging and publishing such remarkable contributions to the knowledge of primitive faiths and institutions.

The American teacher of history should not, however, stop on this side of the world if he would fully understand the significance of the North American Indians. He must compare their religious and social ideas with those of other savages. He must discover the extraordinary resemblance between American forms of spirit worship and ancestor worship with those in ancient Babylonia, in China, and Japan. He must point out the gradual evolution of higher forms of stellar and solar worship. He must show how man began to reverence heavenly powers; how he personified natural forces; how he translated heroes, ancestors, and great kings into celestial deities, and how the divine principle of fatherhood triumphed over and unified all.

There are few subjects of inquiry more fascinating to teachers or to students than the historical evolution of religion and of customary law or government. The history of marriage, as treated by Westermarck, and historical sociology, as presented by such masters as Herbert Spencer, Pustel de Coulanges, McLennan, Morgan, and Sir Henry Maine, are subjects which I have been teaching by lectures to graduate students at the Johns Hopkins University during the present term. I require every student to tabulate the results of his note-taking and private reading in the form of a syllabus suitable for future reference and possible use when the young man becomes a teacher himself. A surprising amount of good materials is thus classified and assimilated. Every student develops his own system of topical arrangement and takes pride in independent work. From the start, note taking on lectures and books becomes vital and self-helpful, instead of a mechanical, perfunctory process. In one of my graduate courses, that on the Nineteenth Century, students have been encouraged each to give a class lecture and submit to a general criticism by his fellows. The course on the Early history of society develops from a study of savage customs into more and more civilized institutions, and ends in a review of Greek politics, historical and theoretical. The course is given to graduates only, and once in three years.

For purposes of graduate training in general history, I have given each year two representative courses of class instruction, one in ancient history and one in modern history. I got the idea from Professor Oncken, of Giessen. All I care to say about the plan is that it works well for purposes of department training. I do not pretend to cover the entire ground. Certain phases only of the subject are presented. Books are recommended and read. Organized quizzes and written examinations do the rest.

It seems to me a mistaken policy for instructors to allow their college students to specialize prematurely in narrow fields of local or even national history, when the great empire of universal history is all undiscovered. For college boys and girls the reading of good selections from a few standard authors on great chapters of the world's civilization yields better educational results than does the close study of historical sources for any given period. Interest may be quickened and the judgment may be trained in historical matters by the comparison of different historians without the expenditure of so much precious time as is required by the study and digest of original sources. It is enough for the ordinary collegian if he is introduced to a few good books of history and politics. It is too much of a burden to load him down with documents and references to archives and sources. The end to be accomplished is historical and political culture, the development of a real interest in the world's life and experience.

The preparation of historical essays is also a good literary means of training collegiate students. They learn by writing to digest the results of private historical reading, but the reading of these essays by the instructor, or the presentation of even the best of them to a class, is wearisome and unprofitable. If a teacher will take pains to mark with care every error of statement or style, he can render a substantial service to his students and thus aid one of his best academic allies—the department of English literature.

Excellent historical results have been secured from undergraduate classes in Baltimore by requiring the students to tabulate their knowledge of certain subjects in thesis form. For example, in institutional history and the history of civilization, college boys, in the second year of their course, have put on record, in brief space, a surprising amount of well-digested material, topically arranged and derived from a comparative study of the best standard authorities. China, Japan, India, Chaldea, Egypt, Phœnicia, and Palestine have been the fields of our study of the history of civilization. The idea is to treat topically and by groups the social, economic, religious, and governmental institutions of the Eastern World, ancient and modern, somewhat as Herbert Spencer and his coworkers have done in their descriptive sociology or groups of sociological facts. The students give references to authorities, which they have actually read, for every statement or group of facts which appear in the written digest. This kind of work is not an essay, but simply a collection of theses or propositions. Materials, thus gathered and arranged, are fairly well assimilated by the student and often prove very suggestive to the teacher. The papers are easily examined, and are sometimes of practical benefit to the class if papers are exchanged or exhibited for a comparison of results. Graduate students at the Johns Hopkins University first acquired this method in undergraduate classes.

After all, the great thing is to interest students in what they are doing, to persuade them that it is worth doing, and that, for the time being and for them, it is the most important work on earth. It is like training for a boat race or a football match. Study becomes an absorbing passion. I have seen old athletes forget their first love, scorn delights, and live laborious days, for the simple sake of reading good books, writing a dissertation, and winning a doctor's degree. One of the reasons why Johns Hopkins graduates cut no figure in athletics is simply this: They have no time to spare for the old familiar games. These men are now training for academic life and professional careers. It is the business of the trainer to keep his men in good condition, and he tries to do it; but, alas! some of them break down and some never arrive at the goal. As in the old Greek torch race, when one man falls another catches the torch and carries it on. "The best master is quickly distanced by the better pupil," says Lord Acton.

"Run, Pheidippides, one race more! the meed is thy due!"

The true function of the teacher of history is to kindle the historical spirit in his pupils, to teach them to know themselves, and to understand the development of mankind historically from the past. "The pupil may become much wiser than his instructor," said Frederic Denison Maurice. "He may not accept his conclusions, but he will own, 'you awakened me to be myself;' for that I thank you."

REMARKS BY PROFESSORS FISHER AND ANDREWS.

Professor FISHER (in the chair): Professor Adams in his paper referred to the advantage of the study of history as including a study of politics in the past, and especially on account of the generic relation of the politics of the past to the present. Perhaps I may be allowed to refer to a remark which I was reminded of made by Dr. Arnold, of Rugby—the additional fact that in the study of ancient life, ancient politics, we have a field where a perfectly dispassionate study of politics is possible. In the midst of the life in which we live, and the political campaigns in which all are so zealously excited, there is a difficulty in that dispassionate and unprejudiced contemplation of political life which is possible in historical study.

Professor ANDREWS. There is always a certain misfortune, perhaps, in following two speakers with whom one so ardently sympathizes as I do; nevertheless there is always testimony which can be stated, even though one follows along in the same line and defends very much the same propositions.

I wonder if, in taking up the subject of teaching history and in defending a certain method, we are not more or less influenced by the peculiar conditions under which we are obliged to work as practical teachers. I happen, for instance, to be one of those unfortunates who is obliged to cover a very large period of time; that is, to instruct my students in as much history as I have time for, whether in covering a period which shall be, in my mind, sufficient to train them and instruct them at the same time. Therefore, naturally I am inclined to advocate, so far as it relates to certain portions of my work, a course of instruction in general history. I propose to limit myself entirely to that phase of the subject,

I can not wholly agree with Professor Burgess's paper. History is more than a residuum. It is the unit, and it is the sum total, which is not merely the sum of all the parts. There may be many different aspects of history, but history in itself considered certainly is something more than those various aspects simply brought into one whole. There is an organic character to history which is something more than a mere summing together. Therefore, if I did not believe that there was such a definition of history, that history were of that character, I certainly should not be able with any conscience to teach as a preliminary course in college that kind of history which I believe to be the history in the largest sense of the word. I can not teach a mere residuum.

History, then, is the organic evolution of peoples. I agree with Professor Emerton, that there is no exact definition which anyone can adopt and defend as against all others. After all, the definition is very like the method. It must be, in some way or other, created by the process of instruction, and I must say that I can only frame my own definition of history by the method which I should employ in instructing students in that which I believe to be most essential for them. Therefore, I would make a plea for, in the early years of a college course, the instructing of students in that general history which alone, I believe, the world is able to give to students—that which they ought to have before them first—on to the higher grades of work. What are such results? What does one seek to attain in such instruction? Something more, I believe, than mere interest. There is something more in historical instruction than the creation of an interest, although that stands very high. There is, I believe, the development in the mind of the student of a sense of criticism; a power of judging as to that which is important and that which is secondary; a power of concentrating all their energy and thought upon those phases of human life which stand out preeminently important and which characterizes a certain age—the age in which they exist. Now, those preeminently important aspects of history are varied according to the characteristics of the period in which the people lived, characterized by a certain degree of intellectual or religious or political or constitutional development. Secondly, I would endeavor to arouse in a class of beginners a judicial sense. That has already been mentioned to-night by Professor Fisher, the chairman. That judicial sense which enables a student to weigh evidence; and not merely weigh evidence for the purpose of bringing out results as an original investigation, but in order to exercise as toward the material used a careful judicial power, which will enable them to compare; not to unduly exaggerate this, or underestimate that, but to act with reason, with common sense, with a mind free from partiality and prejudices, and to draw conclusions which are as near right as human nature is capable of attaining. I do not believe that can be attained by study of the present, and we have to get our first training in a judicial attitude in the past—in that history which does not in any way concern us, either in our politics or religion. Thirdly, I believe that such students should be taught—and perhaps it should stand very high as one of the results of our teaching—a proper sense of perspective and proportion in history, so that they will be able to estimate not only the value of the events of the age as compared with other events of the same age, but will be able to estimate the value and character of one age as compared with the value and character of another age.

History is, as was just stated, an evolution. We can not infuse into an early period ideas, thoughts, and conceptions, either legal, administrative, or constitutional, which belong to the present time, and unless one is led carefully over a large period of time and is given a sufficient amount of historical material to attain to that perspective to see the relation of one period to another, to see how certain phases which are common to us to-day have grown, little by little, out of the past and have become part of the present, unless there be a period of time, such a perspective can hardly be successfully attained. Therefore, I believe and I practice—because I believe it, partly, and because the conditions under which I work are such as to make it necessary, and it makes a difference whether one has the group system or the class system, and this may cover the whole of the years or only one or two years—I believe that the early years of a college course should be given up to work in general history. The question naturally arises: Where is one to begin and where is one to end? I wish it were possible in my own work to follow the suggestion of my old instructor, Dr. Adams, and begin with the Jews, but unfortunately there are time limits, and I have to begin at a later period in order to come down to that which is, after all, the ultimate of all history. The end is the understanding of things as they are to-day.

Now, necessarily, in making good citizens, we teach them a comprehension of the issues of to day in such a way as to interest them. Therefore, I find that about all we can accomplish is to begin with the old Roman Empire and to come down by gradual sequence through the most important of the issues which follow from that time to the present. In that work I believe firmly in the use to the largest extent of illustrative material; that is, that the student should be taught not to depend upon the lecturer or to accept his spoken word as final, but wherever it is possible to be sent, not only to valuable works of the most recent character, whether they be in our own language or any other, whether they be long or short, but to be sent to the original documents, and to be encouraged, just as far as time allows, to read them and to read them carefully. That I believe to be entirely different from Professor Emerton's characterization as top-heavy history. It is not the creation of history. That is a later matter, but it is letting the student gain by a gradual process of familiarity, an acquaintance with the actual written word and the actual appearance, form, and reality of that which is a part and goes to make up history as a whole. Illustrative material I have found to have aided infinitely to the enthusiasm and interest, whereas a mere written lecture would be in itself of only doubtful interest. To give students a document and to have at their own disposal a collection of documents is to give them something that is real, something that has a reality of its own, and brings them pretty closely in contact with the epoch with which the history treats.

REPORT OF PROFESSOR McMASTER'S ADDRESS.

Mr. Chairman, ladies and gentlemen, in the few remarks which I am to have the honor of making this evening I shall endeavor to remember the injunction that a shoemaker should stick to his last. Therefore I will confine myself entirely to the history of our own country. I do that all the more gladly because, coming at the end of such a line of predecessors, I find that is the only history, except that of the Lost Tribes [laughter], which has not been commented upon so far. In presenting it I would like again to say a few words for the great mass of students of history—those, I mean, that get their history in our common schools and stop their instruction there. We know, of course, that the great mass of the thousands of boys and girls that are studying the history of the

United States, almost all of them stop with its text-books and never again obtain any other history of the United States except that which they receive during Presidential campaigns [laughter], or periodically, when some of our Presidents see fit to give the State Department a show.

At the outset of any discussion of this kind, I think we want to draw very clearly a distinction between what we would like to have and what we can get. We have to deal with the practical question: What can we get? At the base of that question is the other question: What do we want, and why do we want it? What is the use, in other words, of a student ever studying the history of the United States? To that there seem to be a vast number of answers, which can be summed up under three heads. Some tell us that the object is that the student ought to know the history of his own country. We are told again that in a nation such as ours, resting as it does upon the vast mass of the people for its stability, it is especially necessary that those whose course runs in the history should have a good knowledge of the history of their own country. And we are told again by others that there is something in history which makes it the only subject which is capable of reasonable, philosophical treatment in order to enable a boy or a girl to distinguish between truth and falsity; hence, to understand that there is such a thing as a temperate and a hasty judgment, and that he or she will revise his or her judgment just as it is seen to be revised by the processes of time.

Now, without going into any discussion as to whether these are good answers or not, we will let them go for what they are worth, and come back to the other question: What can we get? Is it possible to so teach history in our schools all over the country that some real and lasting benefit shall be acquired? That depends upon four elements: First, there is a teacher; second, there is a text-book; third, there is the pupil; fourth, there is the time allowed. With the first two we can deal, but with the student and the time allowed we can not so easily deal. In no course of education is it possible to give to everyone the time that we would like to. Again, we have to deal with the average student rather than with a select few. Those two elements, then, are out of our control. The other two, the text-book and the teacher, are entirely within our control. It is not unreasonable to insist that the teacher of history everywhere should be trained for his work; that the day must pass when the teachers of young boys and girls will be to so large an extent persons who do not intend to make teaching a profession. The time has come when a teacher must be educated for his work. Insisting, then, that the teacher shall be all that he should be, we come to the other question: What can be done with a good teacher with the present text-books? The text-book is far from what it ought to be. It seems to me that it is possible to so present the history of our country to young students, within a limited amount of time, that they can get from it not merely information, but certain fundamental principles which will be of benefit to them and enable them to understand very much better the problems they will have to deal with in later times. It seems to me that it would be better to begin by calling attention to the fact that this country was originally in the possession of a certain number of people of foreign nations; that it has passed, by a certain process, from them to us, and that is about all they need to know of the early colonial history. Then that the Spaniards, for reasons not at all accidental, occupied the Gulf Coast; that the French began their career in Canada, for reasons again perfectly well understood, and that these nations, with the English, were kept apart for a certain period, and that when they came in contact a very trifling incident on Lake Champlain prevented the French from ever getting down on the Middle Atlantic Coast, and that out of that grew matters of vast importance to us. When, afterwards, they were driven far to the westward, that they were brought into contact with such information as enabled them to discover a great river; that the Spaniards, for other reasons perfectly susceptible, were held in the southwest, and that the English then were given an opportunity to develop along the seaboard. Now, with so simple an introduction as that, it is fair to suppose that an ordinary student could understand how the thirteen colonies were organized, and that the English were developing an entirely different form of civilization from that which was being planted by the French in the Mississippi Valley, or by the Spaniards farther to the south. Then there should be presented to the mind of the student the great struggle for the possession of the continent, and that when that ended the first of these great nations disappeared as a nation from our history and its place was taken by the English. Now, then, the student has obtained sufficient knowledge by this time to see how the country which we occupy was populated by these people; how in the course of time they came in conflict, and how out of that conflict resulted the disappearance of one of them and the expansion of the territory of the other. Now comes the struggle between the colonists and the parent country. If that is presented in the proper way the student will obtain a far better knowledge of the instrument, of which none of us know too much, called the Declaration of Independence. That is nothing but the great American Whig platform of the day. Every specification which went in there meant something to the men to whom it appealed. To us it means nothing. The number of persons who could take that instrument up and, beginning with the first charge, specify exactly what that meant, are extremely few. I remember not long ago to have seen an answer to a question which it seemed to me summed it all up. It was a question asked by a teacher: What is the Declaration of Independence? The boy to whom the question was put replied: "It is that part of the book at the back which nobody ever reads." [Laughter.]

Now, if the Declaration of Independence is presented to a student as it should be the student ought to know what those things which were thought to be serious enough to be the cause of a great rebellion meant. Now, then, it seems to me the student is ready for another idea which is not beyond his comprehension. If he is to understand the history of our own country from that day down, he must recognize that when we became independent and free there were along the seaboard three great centers of population, one clustering around Boston as a center, another around Philadelphia and Baltimore, and a third farther south; that each had been founded by people utterly distinct from each other; that the motive which brought them together and the laws and customs which they established were utterly distinct from each other; that when the time came for them to spread westward that they streamed out of these three centers, not in a miscellaneous sort of way, and that they went due west, and that that has been the marked characteristic of emigration so far as we can trace it. If these people had all been alike, the results would probably have been different. Each stream as it passed across the continent planted its own institutions, and it built up a population east and west which to some extent was similar. Then in the course of time events, which it is not necessary to spend much time on or to remind you of, so developed those bands of population that they came to be by the time of the civil war two distinct nations; that there grew up in consequence of that two sets of people who utterly failed to understand each other, and to a large extent do not do so to the present day; that those in the extreme south were in every sense different from those at the extreme north, and we had the division of the country on an east and west line. Now, if attention is called, then, as it can be by the aid of even such maps as are given in the census reports, to that important fact, the student has got another. What use should he make of it? The next fact, I think, should be that while those immense streams of population have been passing westward they have not gone slowly or steadily. Sometimes they have moved with great rapidity, and at other times they have been checked, and the causes which checked them are practically the history of our country since. It is easy enough to understand that when the French Revolution was opened certain conditions were presented to a certain part of the country which enabled them to be the great ocean carriers of the world, and to another part of the country to become the greater producers of the world. That produced such a condition of affairs on the seaboard that the population was stacked up there, and there it remained until that condition had ended. Now, that brings the student down to the war of 1812. By that time an entirely new condition of affairs existed. Then began that rush of population which built up in a few years five cities in the Mississippi Valley. Then something checked it. Then the student has brought to his attention certain ideas which perhaps never occurred to him before. That is, it was possible for such a thing as a canal to cross this State and to produce a condition of affairs which was in itself a great social revolution. The introduction of a new way of doing things and better means of transportation, enabling men to cover a larger field, led to the growth of great cities in the East. Then came a period of hard times, and then the causes for it. The student can be presented with certain ideas which will enable him to understand the history of his country far better, and give him a better idea of the growth of population, and enable him to see that, while our ancestors drew up the famous Declaration of Independence they made something which they could not practice; that at the very time when they were declaring that all men were equal they were forming State constitutions which made them most unequal; and we find, then, in that great instrument—the ordinance of 1787—that these men put into it a kind of government they could not give themselves. Now, it seems to me that in such a way it is possible to do something to improve the general condition of history teaching in our schools. Whether that is done or not rests not upon any individual or body of men, but it rests upon every citizen; and it seems to me that no better use could be made of the opportunities afforded by this Association than to do something toward the improvement of history teaching, not merely in our colleges, but in the common schools of the land, dealing especially with those who come to us from foreign lands, so that they may see the history of our country in such a way that they shall clearly understand it. [Applause.]

CPSIA information can be obtained
at www.ICGtesting.com
Printed in the USA
BVHW041104010219
539257BV00007B/199/P